MW01008442

A TRUE BOOK™

The Wampanoag

KEVIN CUNNINGHAM
AND PETER BENOIT

Children's Press®
An Imprint of Scholastic Inc.
New York Toronto London Auckland Sydney
Mexico City New Delhi Hong Kong
Danbury, Connecticut

Content Consultant
Scott Manning Stevens, PhD
Director, McNickle Center
Newberry Library
Chicago, Illinois

Library of Congress Cataloging-in-Publication Data

Cunningham, Kevin, 1966–
  The Wampanoag/Kevin Cunningham and Peter Benoit.
      p. cm.—(A true book)
  Includes bibliographical references and index.
ISBN-13: 978-0-531-20766-6 (lib. bdg.)   978-0-531-29308-9 (pbk.)
ISBN-10: 0-531-20766-8 (lib. bdg.)   0-531-29308-4 (pbk.)
1. Wampanoag Indians—Juvenile literature. I. Benoit, Peter, 1955– II.Title.
  E99.W2C86 2011
  974.4004'97348—dc22   2010049075

All rights reserved. Published in 2011 by Children's Press, an imprint of Scholastic Inc.
Printed in China 62
SCHOLASTIC, CHILDREN'S PRESS, A TRUE BOOK and associated logos are trademarks and/or registered trademarks of Scholastic Inc.

1 2 3 4 5 6 7 8 9 10 R 19 18 17 16 15 14 13 12 11

Find the Truth!

Everything you are about to read is true *except* for one of the sentences on this page.

Which one is **TRUE**?

T or F The severed head of a Wampanoag chief was displayed on a pole for more than 20 years.

T or F The Wampanoag lived in teepees.

Find the answers in this book.

3

Contents

THE BIG TRUTH!

Making the Wetu

Squanto, a Wampanoag warrior and translator

A wetu, a traditional Wampanoag dwelling

The first English settlers of Plimouth were first referred to as "the Pilgrims" in the 1800s.

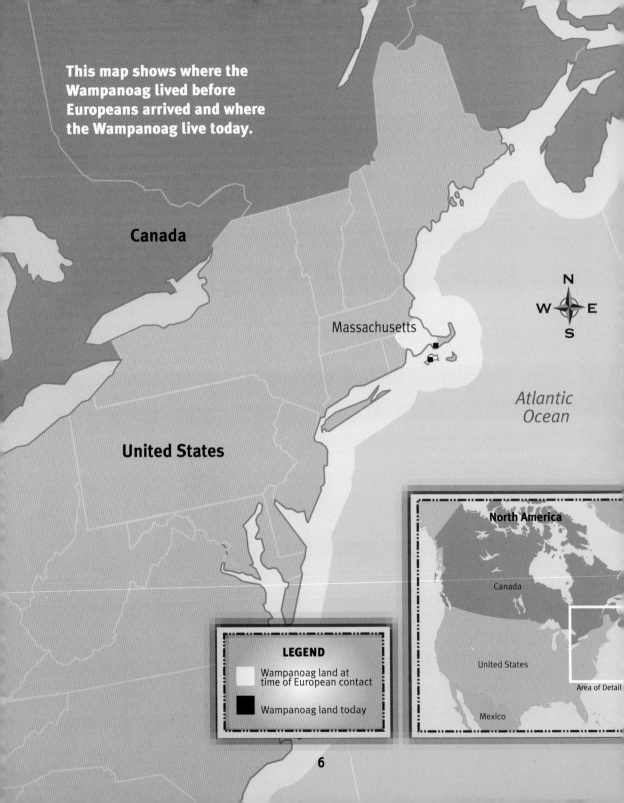

This map shows where the Wampanoag lived before Europeans arrived and where the Wampanoag live today.

Canada

Massachusetts

United States

Atlantic Ocean

N
W   E
S

LEGEND
Wampanoag land at time of European contact
Wampanoag land today

North America

Canada

United States

Area of Detail

Mexico

CHAPTER 1

A Place in History

The Wampanoag lived in what are today Rhode Island and eastern Massachusetts. According to their **tradition**, they had been there since the dawn of time. Scientists believe the Wampanoag arrived sometime after the last ice age. By 1000 C.E., they had borrowed ideas such as farming from a Midwestern culture called the Hopewell. Later, the Wampanoag enjoyed an **alliance** with their neighbors the Massachusett and Nauset peoples.

 The word *Wampanoag* means "People of the First Light," or "People of the Dawn."

Strangers off the Coast

In 1524, the Wampanoag made contact with Europeans who had traveled across the Atlantic Ocean. Giovanni da Verrazzano, an Italian explorer working for France, sailed his ship *Dolphin* into a bay in present-day Rhode Island. From there, he traded goods with local Wampanoag. Fishing boats and traders soon followed Verrazzano's lead. One type of "goods" Europeans wanted was slaves. They kidnapped Wampanoag and enslaved them to work in Europe.

Giovanni da Verrazzano landed in what is today's Newport Harbor in Rhode Island.

Squanto

In 1614, slave trader Thomas Hunt captured about 20 Wampanoag and sold some of them in Spain. One of the slaves, Squanto, had trained to become a special advisor-warrior for the **sachem**, or chief, in Patuxet, his home village. The training included learning to ignore pain by doing painful things, not eating for long periods, and forcing himself to throw up over and over.

The Wampanoag called an advisor-warrior a *pniese* (pah-NEES).

Squanto is remembered for helping Europeans who settled in the Northeast.

Squanto returned to Patuxet on his second trip from Europe to North America.

Squanto's knowledge of English was valuable as more white settlers moved into Wampanoag territory.

Once in Spain, Squanto convinced his owners to let him return home. His training helped him deal with struggles on the way. In London, he learned English working for a shipbuilder named John Slany. When Slany sailed to America, he took Squanto with him as a **translator**. Squanto soon joined explorers heading south along the coast. When he arrived outside Patuxet in 1619, however, he saw an awful sight. His people were gone.

Death Among the Wampanoag

In 1616, an **epidemic** had struck native peoples along the coast. Some experts think smallpox and other diseases killed nine out of every ten Wampanoag. As Squanto wandered the region, he saw entire villages empty of people. But the Wampanoag who remained soon faced another threat. Because so few of them had lived, they could not defend their lands against other native peoples hit less hard by the disease.

Smallpox and other diseases, brought by the Europeans, killed huge numbers of Wampanoag and other native people.

11

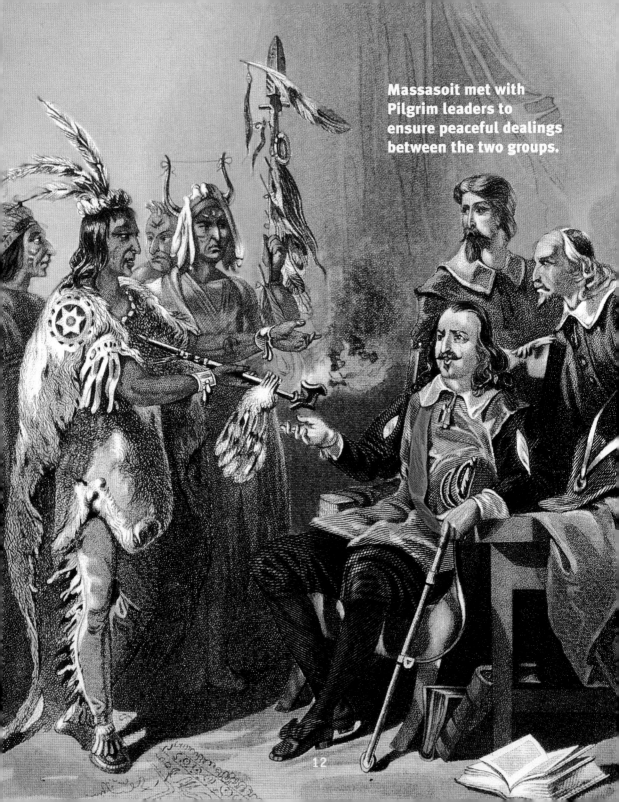

Massasoit met with Pilgrim leaders to ensure peaceful dealings between the two groups.

CHAPTER **2**

The Wampanoag and the English

The Wampanoag who survived banded together under a sachem named Massasoit. Because of the epidemic, they had to give up lands to the Narragansett, the people living to the west. Soon, outsiders came from the other direction. Europeans had returned to settle permanently. Massasoit had dealt with Europeans before. In 1603, his father had driven away a group of English explorers.

A visiting English settler helped Massasoit recover from a dangerous illness in 1623.

13

The Pilgrims

The European settlers, called Pilgrims, were fleeing religious **persecution** in England. After their ship the *Mayflower* dropped anchor in today's Provincetown Harbor, the Pilgrims explored the nearby area. There they found empty native villages and farms. They also ran into angry Wampanoag who shot at them with bows and arrows. The loud English guns surprised the native warriors and drove them into the woods—for a while.

Before 1620, the *Mayflower* had transported wine, not people.

The Pilgrims reached land in November 1620.

Arriving just as winter was beginning, the Pilgrims struggled to construct a village in the new land.

Hard Times

In the meantime, the settlers faced illness and hunger. They simply had no idea how to live in the new land. Almost half the Pilgrims died during the winter. The rest survived by digging up food the Wampanoag had buried years earlier. In March 1621, the settlers finished turning empty Patuxet into a town they called New Plimoth. Massasoit soon sent them a message. To their shock, the sachem's messenger spoke English. It was Squanto.

A Deal

Squanto, acting as a translator, helped Massasoit work out a **treaty** that gave the English about 12,000 acres (4,900 hectares). In return, the English helped the Wampanoag fight the Narragansett. Squanto stayed on to teach the settlers how to grow maize (corn), beans, and squash, and where to find the best hunting and fishing. Other area peoples, especially the Narragansett, disliked the treaty. Whenever they attacked the Wampanoag, the English fought for Massasoit's people.

Squanto called himself *Tisquantum*, meaning "great anger."

Squanto taught the settlers a lot that helped them survive not only their first winter, but long after that.

The First "Thanksgiving"

In October 1621, the English settlers decided to hold a celebration in honor of a successful harvest. Ninety-one Wampanoag attended the three-day event. They brought venison (deer meat). The English supplied ducks and geese, as well as samp, a stew made from ground maize. The Wampanoag and settlers also played games and danced. The modern holiday we now call Thanksgiving was inspired by that harvest feast.

The tradition of Thanksgiving was made official when President Abraham Lincoln declared it a holiday in 1863.

17

Plimoth Grows

The Pilgrims began having less and less control over their **colony**. Newcomers arriving in Plimoth saw no reason to get along with the native peoples and soon pushed them off their land. The new settlers brought more diseases. They also tried to turn the Wampanoag into Christians with English ways. Massasoit resisted, but the English plan was working. His sons even gave themselves English names. Wamsutta became King Alexander, and Metacom became King Philip.

More than 500 Pequots died in the Mystic Massacre, in Mystic, Connecticut, ending the Pequot War.

Wamsutta's death left the position of sachem open for Metacom.

King Philip's War

The colony's leaders came to fear Wamsutta's power among his people. They summoned the new sachem to a meeting. The settlers held him prisoner for three days. Soon after leaving for home, he fell ill and died. Metacom believed the English had poisoned his brother. He took over as sachem and asked other tribes for support to stop the settlers from taking native lands.

Metacom effectively ended the peace his father had kept with the Pilgrims.

A Native American man spying for the English may have warned the colonists of Metacom's plans. When the spy was murdered in June 1675, the colonial government put three Wampanoag on trial for the crime. The three were put to death. Native warriors from several tribes raided English towns in revenge. The English, in turn, attacked the villages of the Wampanoag, Narragansett, and others. King Philip's War soon exploded into a bloody conflict.

During the two-year war, Native American warriors attacked half of the 90 or so English settlements. The English wiped out entire native villages and sold prisoners into slavery. Around 3,000, or 40 percent, of the Indian population died. Only 400 Wampanoag survived. Other tribes vanished forever. In the end, English troops captured Metacom, cut off his head, and displayed it on a pole outside Plimoth for more than 20 years.

About 600 English settlers were killed in the war.

The Three Sisters were important to the diet of many native peoples.

CHAPTER 3

Wampanoag Culture

Wampanoag men and women had clear roles in everyday life. Men hunted and fished. Women gathered nuts and berries and also farmed. Wampanoag farmers depended on the **Three Sisters**—maize, beans, and squash. Maize stalks provided a pole for bean plants to wrap around. The leafy squash vines protected soil from battering rains. Maize, meanwhile, gave a farming community more food per acre than any other **cereal** on Earth.

 Maize was bred from central Mexico's teosinte grass.

A Boy's Life

Boys learned to hunt and fish at a young age. Around age two, they began to shoot a bow. As young men, they dodged arrows shot by friends. During the summer, boys were sent to camp in the maize fields to keep the birds away and pull weeds. The Wampanoag male took a test of manhood in his teens. For one winter, he lived in the forest with nothing except a bow, hatchet, and knife.

Tools were often made from wood and stone, including this axe (left), club (center), and adze (right), a woodworking tool.

Wetus were designed to be taken apart and reconstructed quickly and easily.

What Girls Learned

Girls farmed with their mothers and learned to tend the Wampanoag house, called a **wetu**. Women could take down and put together a wetu in a few hours. This was important because the Wampanoag moved short distances for summer and then back again for winter. Women as well as men told stories, sang, and carved shapes out of wood and seashells. They also used plants and animal parts for healing.

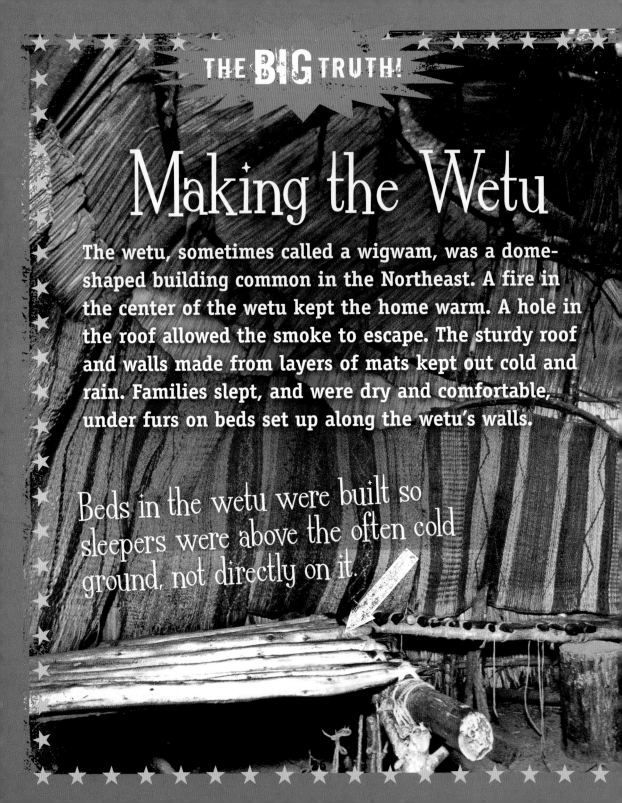

Making the Wetu

The wetu, sometimes called a wigwam, was a dome-shaped building common in the Northeast. A fire in the center of the wetu kept the home warm. A hole in the roof allowed the smoke to escape. The sturdy roof and walls made from layers of mats kept out cold and rain. Families slept, and were dry and comfortable, under furs on beds set up along the wetu's walls.

Beds in the wetu were built so sleepers were above the often cold ground, not directly on it.

The Dome Shape

Men created a dome-shaped frame by cutting down and bending 100 or so saplings. Sturdy strips of tree bark were used to tie the saplings together.

The Walls

The Wampanoag sewed cattails into two-sided mats that covered the outside of the sapling frame. Inside, they put up a second layer of mats made from a water plant called the bulrush.

Weatherproof

The English wondered how wetus stayed so dry. Rain, sleet, and snow ran off the wetu's domed shape. Many modern-day tents borrow the wetu's design in order to keep campers dry and warm.

The Sachems

Although influential, the sachems, or chiefs, had limited power over a Wampanoag band. This was common among Native American peoples. Rather than just giving orders, the leader made agreements with the important people in his tribe and with other leaders. A bad sachem paid a price. Families or villages unhappy with him might move away or become loyal to another sachem. When they did, he lost respect.

Modern-day Wampanoag sachems, such as Vernon "Silent Drum" Lopez (left), still support their tribes through dealings with tribe members and outsiders, including the U.S. government.

As grand sachem, Massasoit was in charge of relations with the Pilgrims for all associated Wampanoag groups.

On rare occasions, women served as sachems.

A sachem had many responsibilities. He or she made treaties with other peoples, decided when to go to war, enforced laws, and settled disagreements over land. A sachem swore loyalty to a more powerful leader called the great sachem. Sometimes a son followed his father as sachem, as Wamsutta did after Massasoit died. But it was possible for others to become sachems without that connection.

A daughter could inherit a wetu from her mother.

A family's land gave them space to build a wetu and grow crops.

Owning Land

The Wampanoag **inherited** land through the mother's family. A mother always gave the land to her daughters. Men got land through marriage. Though most Native American men had only one wife, the Wampanoag allowed a man to have more. Because women owned the property, a man might take two or more wives to control a large amount of land. Land added to his wealth and power.

The Wampanoag at War

The Wampanoag fought with outsiders such as the Narragansett, the Pequot, and European settlers. But they also fought with each other. Usually, a battle started because of an insult or because a sachem wished to gain respect. Two groups of warriors crept in the forest, shot it out with bows and arrows, and left when one side had won. The losing Wampanoag band always admitted it had lost. To not do so was considered wrong.

Wampanoag warriors began training from boyhood.

An English village in Massachusetts is attacked by Native Americans during King Philip's War.

Weetamoo the Sachem

Weetamoo was the best known of the Wampanoag's female sachems. When her first husband died, Weetamoo married Massasoit's son Wamsutta. She was about 27 when Wamsutta died after his meeting with Plimoth's leaders. Afterward, she went to Metacom to ask for his help. Metacom declared war on the English to protect his sister-in-law's honor as well as to fight against settlers taking Wampanoag land.

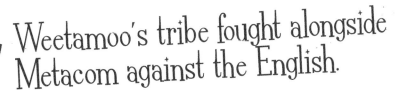

Weetamoo's tribe fought alongside Metacom against the English.

Mary Rowlandson's Story

Historians have a firsthand account of Weetamoo from the writings of Mary Rowlandson, an English settler. On February 10, 1675, the Wampanoag and their allies burned down the village of Lancaster, Massachusetts. The attackers captured Rowlandson and her three children. For 11 weeks, they were held prisoner by Quinnapin, whom Weetamoo would soon marry. Eventually, Rowlandson's husband paid for the return of Mary and their two surviving children.

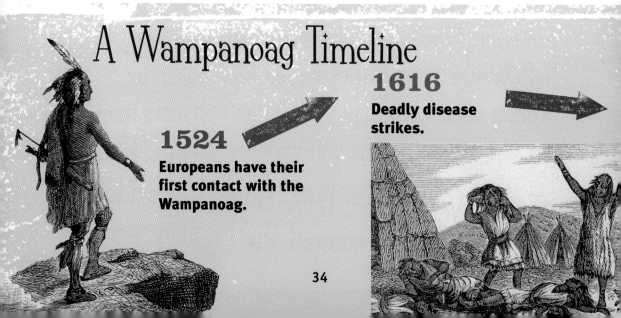

A Wampanoag Timeline

1524

Europeans have their first contact with the Wampanoag.

1616

Deadly disease strikes.

Rowlandson said of Weetamoo, "A severe and proud dame she was." Though Weetamoo hated the English, the Wampanoag had taken up many English customs over the previous fifty years. Weetamoo wore makeup and powdered her hair in the style of English ladies she had known. Rowlandson also noticed how much Weetamoo liked necklaces, earrings, and other jewelry.

1620
Pilgrims arrive.

1675–1676
King Philip's War is fought.

The End of the War

Weetamoo had no patience for men who wanted to deal with the English. By the end of the war, she had left both Quinnapin and a fourth husband. When the English finally captured Metacom, Weetamoo had to run for her life. She drowned trying to cross the Taunton River. The settlers placed her head on a pole in Taunton, Massachusetts.

Weetamoo's hopes for defeating the English settlers ended with the capture and death of Metacom.

Popular Stories

A captivity story was a narrative about a white person held prisoner, or captive, by Native Americans. Mary Rowlandson's book, first published in 1682, was one of the most popular of these stories. Many white readers learned all they knew about Native Americans from such books. Most stories, however, gave readers a wrong picture of Native Americans because the authors made up details to make native peoples look bad or to make the story more exciting.

Rowlandson's story of her capture became a best-seller.

THE
NARRATIVE
OF THE
CAPTIVITY AND RESTORATION
OF
Mrs. Mary Rowlandson,

Who was taken Prisoner by the INDIANS with several others, and treated in the most barbarous and cruel Manner by those vile Savages : With many other remarkable Events during her TRAVELS.

Written by her own Hand, for her private Use, and now made public at the earnest Desire of some Friends, and for the Benefit of the afflicted.

Wampanoag traditions are kept alive through ceremonies and festivals.

CHAPTER 5

Voices From the Past

Diseases continued to kill many of the Wampanoag. During the American Revolution, some Wampanoag men fought alongside the colonists. Most of them died. Women had to marry men from other native groups. Over time, fewer people spoke the Wampanoag language and more used English.

In the last few years, modern-day Wampanoag have begun to offer Wampanoag lessons to save their language from dying out. One group is putting together a Wampanoag dictionary.

Language is one way to hold on to an important part of Wampanoag culture. Another way the culture lives on is through folklore. In the heart of the Wampanoags' former lands in southeastern Massachusetts lies a region of almost 200 square miles (500 square kilometers) called the Bridgewater Triangle. Much of King Philip's War was fought in the Triangle. There are ancient cemeteries there. People have told stories about this historically rich area for hundreds of years.

Metacom and Weetamoo are both said to have used Hockomock Swamp in the Triangle as a hiding place.

Many have claimed to see the legendary creature Bigfoot in the Bridgewater Triangle. ➡️

The Freetown-Fall River State Forest lies in the Triangle. The Wampanoag sold the forest to the English settlers 350 years ago. It is said the Wampanoag cursed the forest, as well as nearby Hockomock Swamp. The swamp is where Metacom and his warriors hid during King Philip's War. For centuries, people in both areas have reported seeing mysterious lights, ghosts, and a giant bird.

Today, the Wampanoag number a little more than 2,000. Their part in American history continues to have a powerful hold on the imagination. Every Thanksgiving, for example, Americans relive a time when Wampanoag villages dotted the landscape. They remember when the native men and women living there taught the English settlers to survive. Though the Wampanoag language is only now reappearing, the Wampanoag's ways and actions have always been a part of our country's history. ★

A group of Mashpee Wampanoags celebrate together.

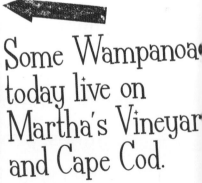

Some Wampanoag today live on Martha's Vineyard and Cape Cod.

True Statistics

Number of Wampanoag in 1600: About 12,000

Number of Wampanoag captured with Squanto: About 20

Percentage of Wampanoag who died of disease from 1616 to 1619: Up to 90 percent

Amount of land Massasoit gave to the English: 12,000 acres (4,900 ha)

Number of Wampanoag at the First Thanksgiving: 91

Number of Indians killed in King Philip's War: 3,000

Number of English killed in King Philip's War: 600

Number of Wampanoag in 1677: About 400

Number of saplings in a wetu dome: Up to 100

Amount of time Mary Rowlandson was held prisoner: 11 weeks

Area of Bridgewater Triangle: 200 sq. mi. (500 sq km)

Number of Wampanoag today: About 2,000

Did you find the truth?

(T) The severed head of a Wampanoag chief was displayed on a pole for more than 20 years.

(F) The Wampanoag lived in teepees.

Resources

Books

Bial, Raymond. *The Wampanoag*. New York: Benchmark, 2004.

DeKeyser, Stacy. *The Wampanoag*. New York: Children's Press, 2005.

Dell, Pamela. *The Wampanoag*. New York: Marshall Cavendish, 2008.

Gray-Kanatiiosh, Barbara A. *Wampanoag*. Edina, MN: Checkerboard Books, 2004.

Hirschfelder, Arlene R. *Squanto*. Mankato, MN: Blue Earth Books, 2003.

Levy, Janey. *The Wampanoag of Massachusetts and Rhode Island*. New York: PowerKids Press, 2005.

Riehecky, Janet. *The Wampanoag: People of the First Light*. Mankato, MN: Bridgestone Books, 2003.

Organizations and Web Sites

Boston Children's Museum: The Wampanoag

www.bostonkids.org/educators/wampanoag/html/
w-origins.htm
Read the words of the Wampanoag as they talk about their origins
and history.

Wampanoag Tribe of Gay Head

www.wampanoagtribe.net/pages/wampanoag_acc/who
Learn about Wampanoag history and see what's going on today in
a Wampanoag community in Massachusetts.

Places to Visit

National Museum of the American Indian

National Mall
Fourth Street & Independence
Ave., SW
Washington, DC 20560
(202) 633-1000
www.nmai.si.edu
View exhibits about the
lives and cultures of
Native Americans.

Plimoth Plantation

137 Warren Avenue
Plymouth, MA 02360
(508) 746-1622
www.plimoth.org
Visit a historical village that
shows what life was like for
the Wampanoag and English
settlers in the 1600s.

Important Words

alliance (uh-LYE-uhnss) — a number of groups working together

cereal (SIHR-ee-uhl) — plants (like wheat and maize) that provide grains that can be eaten

colony (KAH-luh-nee) — a group of people living in a new place

epidemic (ep-uh-DEM-ik) — a disease that makes a large number of people sick

inherited (in-HER-it-ed) — received something from a parent or other relative after the relative's death

persecution (pur-suh-KYU-shun) — being treated harshly for holding certain beliefs or belonging to certain groups

sachem (SAY-chum) — chief

Three Sisters (THREE SISS-turz) — maize, beans, and squash grown together

tradition (truh-DISH-uhn) — a pattern of thought or action passed down from one generation to the next

translator (TRANS-late-ur) — a person who takes the words of one language and changes them into the words of another

treaty (TREE-tee) — an agreement or deal

wetu (WE-tu) — a domed house built of saplings and mats woven of plants

Index

Page numbers in **bold** indicate illustrations

About the Authors

Kevin Cunningham has written more than 40 books on disasters, the history of disease, Native Americans, and other topics. Cunningham lives near Chicago with his wife and young daughter.

Peter Benoit is educated as a mathematician but has many other interests. He has taught and tutored high school and college students for many years, mostly in math and science. He also runs summer workshops for writers and students of literature. Benoit has written more than 2,000 poems. His life has been one committed to learning. He lives in Greenwich, New York.